The best guide of

Zakynthos

with 160 coloured photographs

ZANTE

ATHENS

Publisher:
Stelios Kontaratos
Iakovos Kontaratos

Texts:
Eleni Daskalaki

Photographs:
Loukas Chapsis
George Vdokakis
Pantelis Voukouris

Artistic Editing:
N. Vagias

Translation:
Avraam Loucaides – A-Z Services

Copyright©: **Summer Dream Editions**

32, AEROPIS Str. 118 52 ATHENS, GREECE
TEL.: ++30-210-34 50 471 FAX: ++30-210-34 59 114

ISBN: 978-960-7439-58-1

Zakynthos

*The best guide with
160 coloured photographs*

HISTORY – CIVILIZATION – ARTS
FOLKLORE – EXCURSIONS – ROAD MAPS

Summer Dream EDITIONS

CONTENTS

Introduction

With its lace-like beaches, green hillsides and fertile lowlands, its stately town and distinctive villages, Zakynthos is one of the favourite islands in the Ionian Sea.

The island of the renowned poets, Solomos and Kalvos, and the theatrical playwright, Gregorios Xenopoulos, was a cradle of civilization even during the most difficult periods of Greek history.

With its distinctive and diverse churches and belfries that soar into the sky, chanting the works of God and man, the old mansions, the arches in the narrow alleyways and the widespread squares, Zakynthos enchants even the most demanding visitor.

The book that you are holding in your hands was compiled with love for Zakynthos in order to guide you –together with your personal preferences– to learn about and to enjoy this green-filled island situated in the Ionian Sea.

Enjoy your holidays!!

A flashback to the history of Zakynthos

Zakynthos, as with all the other islands in the Ionian Sea, played a significant role in the history of Europe, due to its key geographical position in the Mediterranean and the European continent. Due to their geographical position, the Ionian Islands were always the apple of discord for many races, even way back in Antiquity. Thus the history of Zakynthos is rich in events and successive conquests by various races that differed only in their nationality, leading up to the island's unification with the remaining Greece on 21st May 1864.

From Antiquity to the Byzantine Era

Mycaenean graves in Kambi

The **first signs of life** on Zakynthos date back to the Neolithic Period and were found in the Bay of Laganas, where petrified bones from the Paeloliothic Era were also discovered at the same time. Various findings and the testimonies of ancient writers tell us that during the period of Antiquity a notable civilization flourished on Zakynthos, but not many specimens however have been discovered –possibly due to the many catastrophic earthquakes– so as to

An island with many names

The island of Zakynthos was first mentioned during the time of Homer. According to Homer, the island's "god-father" was Zakynthos, who was its first settler and the son of Dardanos, who came to the island from the Arkadian town of Psofida around 1500-1600 B.C. These first settlers, once they fortified the acropolis of the island, named the island Psofida in order to honour and to remember their homeland. Another name for Zakynthos that is also referred to by Homer is Yliessa, which means "forest land". At various periods of times Zakynthos was also called Diakynthos, Diakythos, Iakynthos, Zakita, Jacinthum, Jantes, Lesande, etc., obviously using various paraphrases of its name.

allow us to have a more complete picture of the island's past. During the years that followed the colonization of the island by Zakynthos and the creation of colonies on islands in the Aegean, as well as in various regions in the Mediterranean, Zakynthos was conquered by Arkisios, King of Cephallinia. The island later passed to Odysseus, son of Laertes, King of Ithaca.

Its geographical position, fertile soil and coal tar resources helped the island to develop economically. The **Persian Wars** found Zakynthos to be sometimes neutral and sometimes an ally of the Lacedaemonians, and later as a member of the Athenian Alliance. The following period that included the **Macedonian Wars** and

The two-storied Cave of Damianos in Agalas with its stalactites and stalagmites

the campaigns of Phillip on Greek land finds Zakynthos falling into the hands of the Macedonians and later the Romans, until the island is finally incorporated into the Roman District of Achaia is 146 B.C., together with Epirus, the Peloponnese and the islands of the Aegean, except for Crete.

Other than the initial years of the **Roman domination** when Roman Vice-Consuls governed the island, Zakynthos acquired relative autonomy and had its own municipality, parliament, legislation and currency with a separate symbol. The spreading of Christianity reached Zakynthos during the period after the Mithridatian Wars. The political scene in the Ionian changed during the years following the decline of the Roman Empire and the concurrent rise and domination of the Byzantine Era, and Zakynthos was initially incorporated into the province of Illyria and later became part of the 11th Province of Longovardia, with Ravena in Italy as its capital. In 887 A.D. the island was finally incorporated into the Province of Cephallinia, along with the other Ionian Islands.

Roman Zakynthian coin dating back to the 2nd C. B.C.

Zakynthian "statiras" – 5th C. B.C.

The domination of the West

During the period of the **Crusades,** the island was again subjected to looting and desolation by the Norman Voimondo, who attacked the Ionian Islands with great savagery. Zakynthos was finally conquered by the Venetians during the IVth Crusade and was incorporated – together with Cephalonia- into the Principality of Achaia.

The Venetians were followed by the French who claimed the Ionian Islands in order to dominate the trading and economy in the region. From the end of the 12th C. up to 1357, Zakynthos was ruled by the Italian Orsini family, who ceded it ecclesiastically to Pope Innocentio the

The spring of Herodotos

The region of Dodeka Pigadia (=Twelve Wells) in Agalas, constructed in the 15th C. by the Venetians

Third of Rome. The marriage that followed –which united the Orsini dynasty with the De Tocchi family– only changed the name of the Governor of Zakynthos, and this rule continued with only a brief interval when Zakynthos passed into the hands of the Sultan of the **Ottoman Empire.**

In 1452 Leonardo the Second of the De Tocchi family reinstated the Orthodox Bishopric of Cephalonia and Zakynthos and restored the Orthodox Bishop, thus satisfying the wishes of the people for religious tolerance.

The prosperity and good relations of the governor with the local inhabitants cannot however withstand the mania of Kapoudan Pasha, who overran the Ionian Islands, but in 1485 the Venetians prevail in the diplomatic game with the Turks and regain Zakynthos on condition that they pay 500 ducats to the Sultan every year. The families of the **Venetian nobles** that established themselves on the island during the years that followed acquired titles and honours and their family names were recorded in the "Golden Bible" of the island's nobility – the renowned **Libro d' Oro.**

Lithography depicting Ag. Markos Square (Cartwright, 1863)

During the general climate of economic prosperity and security, the town of Zakynthos (called Egialos) soon surpassed the limiting borders of the Kastro (=Castle) and spreads out towards the sea. The town is "adorned" with large squares and beautiful buildings, roads are demarked and the Venetians call Zakynthos the "Florence of Greece".

In 1499 the Venetian-Turkish conflict breaks out which suddenly suspends this peaceful period and Zakynthos becomes a replenishment port for the Venetian and French navies. During the second phase –the Kingdom of Suleiman– the Venetian-Turkish War is rekindled and Zakynthos again goes through a period of looting and besiegement by pirates.

After the end of the wars and the restoration of peace, an event takes place that is significant in European history. The local bourgeoisie and the populace revolt against the nobility in this first (for that period of time)

urban populace revolution in Europe and became known as **"Rebellion of the Populace or Rabble"** (1628-1632). This action is finally repressed but life on the island does not carry on peacefully during the troubled years that Europe was going though. When there were no wars or attacks by the enemy, the life of the inhabitants was threatened by deadly pestilences or epidemics.

During the **Cretan War** (1645-1669) the Ionian Islands played a leading role in the battles against the Turks. The Venetians finally drew up a treaty with the Turks, ceding to them the ownership of the island of Crete in exchange

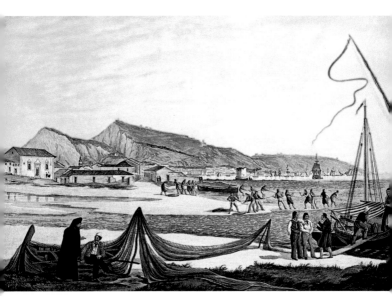

Lithography depicting the harbour and the town of Zakynthos (Cartwright, 1863)

for not paying tax for the occupation of Zakynthos. Thus many Cretans fled to Zakynthos in order to avoid the Turks and Cretan civilization finds fertile soil on the island, thus giving a new impetus to the cultural development of Zakynthos. A second wave of migrants –this time from the Peloponnese- takes refuge on Zakynthos after the failure of the nationalist-liberal movement that was instigated in 1770 by Catherine the Second of Russia, known as "Orlofika".

The reverberations of the French Revolution in 1789 reaches the Ionian Islands and their inhabitants, affected and encouraged, sought social equality, self-rule and justice. In June 1797 the flag of the French democrats is raised panegyrically at the Kastro on Zakynthos. The inhabitants, believing that a new page in their history had been tuned, burn the "Golden Bible" of the nobility and symbolically planted the "Tree of Freedom" in the Square of Agios Markos.

Within this framework of fair and just governing, the French formed the "Presidency of the Town Hall" without the participation of the nobles; they abolished the titles of the nobility and assigned the administration of the island to committees composed of the bourgeois or townsmen, farmers and the populari. Zakynthos became the headquarters of the "Aegean Sea Prefecture" and schools were established on the island for the children of all its citizens.

However, despite these positive movements it was not easy to resolve all the economical and social problems that had accumulated during the passing years and in addition, the French had to deal with problems caused by the nobility, who attempted to create a state of anarchy on the island and to overturn the new status quo. The British blockage that followed made matters even worse, and the result was that the French remained on Zakynthos for only 15 months.

The formation of the Ionian State

The alliance of powerful Russia with the Ottoman Empire delivers the final blow to the liberal French, who keep some of the eastern countries in Europe. With them stand the nobility, who try to reinstate oligarchy. Thus, at a time when the Russo-Turkish fleet is besieging Zakynthos and the French are defending it, some of the local leaders symbolically hand over the keys of the town to the Russians, thus forcing the French garrison to surrender in October 1798. To ensure their privileges, the nobility turn to oligarchic England and ask for their assistance so as not to lose their privileges again.

In March of 1800 the first so-called independent Greek State is formed – the **Ionian (Eptanesian) State**. This initiative belonged to Russia and

An icon of the Virgin Mary in the Museum of Byzantine Art

Turkey. In reality this independence was of course a mere formality since the Russians had the main say in governing the island while the State paid an annual tax to Turkey. This regime rouses the Zakynthians who were worn out from the successive conquerors, and the people rebelled. The democratic politician, Antonios Martinengos, organises a movement and declares Zakynthos to be independent of the Ionian State, and he raises the British flag in the Kastro on Zakynthos in order to win the support of a major power. However, the Great Powers again play their own political games and in negotiations with the British, the Turks reinstate Zakynthos into the Ionian State up to 1807. For the next two years the French imperialists retake Zakynthos and they in turn are followed by the British in September 1809.

Agios Georgios of Filikon

British domination – The establishment of the Friendly Society

The British occupation period left its mark on the administration and organization of Zakynthos. They constructed infrastructure works such as aqueducts and roads and a part of the port is still being used.

Repair-work on public buildings and churches in the town were also carried out, and public health was organized. A significant cultural event was the establishment of the public printer which among others printed the "Newspaper of the Liberated Islands".

In 1814 it was decided to form the autonomous **"United States of the Ionian Islands"**, where the British essentially retained administration by appointing their own Resident Commissioner for Zakynthos.

In the meantime, the idea of a free and united Greece began to evolve and the first seeds were laid, the most significant being the establishment of the Friendly Society in Fanari in Constantinople. In December 1818 the **Friendly Society** moves to Zakynthos and its members give an oath of allegiance for the motherland at the Church of Ag. Georgios situated in Psiloma above the town, the first being Theodoros Kolokotronis.

The monument of Filikon

In the years that followed, many Zakynthians passed over to the Peloponnese to fight next to their fellow Greek countrymen. Despite the initial objections of the British, Zakynthos will evolve into a centre for Anglophile revolutionaries who seek British protection in order to support the revolution.

The ruined Monastery of the Virgin Mary of Skopiotissas

Unification with Greece

A requirement for the liberation and independence of a nation is to ensure education and this is exactly what took place on Zakynthos during the years that Greece was fighting for its independence. In 1832 the island had 37 schools while in 1836 the first private school opened, which taught Greek, Italian, History and other basic subjects.

The creation of a liberated Greek State encourages the attempts of the Ionian Islands to achieve independence and their unification with the remaining part of Greece. The free spirit of the Zakynthians cannot be subdued any more. Even before freedom of the press is allowed on the island, the first newspapers began to circulate and in 1849 the **"Foskolos" cultural society** is formed.

In the meantime, politicians and scholars from the Ionian Islands begin to pressurise the British to withdraw their protection from the Ionian Islands, while in 1851 the parliamentarian Ioannis Typaldos-Kapeletos proposes the passing of a resolution by the Ionian Parliament for the unification of the Ionian Islands with Greece. The British replied with harsh reprisals. In

Venetian tap at Kryoneri

December 1858 W.E. Gladstone, an emissary from Queen Victoria and a Phil-Hellenist, arrives on Zakynthos in order to study the Ionian matter, while everything points to the fact that England is ready to settle this matter. In exchange for the enthroning of George the First –the Danish prince who is being promoted by the English courtyard– England will cede the Ionian Islands to the Greek State.

The Greek flag is raised at the Kastro on Zakynthos on 21st May 1864, thus creating a wave of emotion and enthusiasm among the inhabitants. About two months later the Zakynthians will welcome the new King of Greece to their island, and after eons of foreign occupation the Ionian Islands finally unite their future with that of the remaining parts of Greece and in continuation, a common historical course.

The old bridge of Argasio built in 1803

*The old
Sarakinas
mansion*

Arts and Civilization

Picture exhibited in the Skevofylakio Museum depicting the Monastery of Strofadon and Agios Dionysios

Zakynthos, as with the other islands in the Ionian Sea, showed significant intellectual and cultural development quite early because it was directly influenced by the civilization that was spreading in Western Europe. During the last years of the successive conquests by the French and the Italians, and especially after unification with the remaining part of Greece, both civilization and artistry prospers on the island. Thus Zakynthos becomes an important centre for Post-Byzantine art, a centre for the development of music, historical research and lyrical poetry. Renowned men of the letters such as **Martelaos, Kalvos, Tertsetis, Tsakasianos, Zois, Xenopoulos** and **Matesis,** gave us notable works, theatrical plays that laid the foundations for the Neo-Hellenic theatre, novels that comprised the starting point for Neo-Hellenic prose. At the same time **Pavlos Karrer** gave us the first Greek melodrama, "Markos Botsaris".

The **earthquakes** in August 1953 and the fires that subsequently followed unfortunately destroyed all that which for centuries had expressed the cultural traditions of the island. The reconstruction of the town of Zakynthos responded in part to the architectural tradition of the island, but it could not restore the atmosphere and ambience of the old town that had been formulated by the passing centuries.

The theatre also flourished significantly on Venetian-occupied Zakynthos, with influences from the Italian populist theatre of the Middle-Ages and the Renaissance. The love of the Zakynthians for caustic wit and satire leads to the development of the idiosyncratic Zakynthian theatrical form – speeches. An important role in the

The poet Dionysios Solomos

development of theatrical speech was played by the inter-mixing of the Zakynthian population with the refugees from Crete, who settled on the Ionian Islands after the destruction of Handaka, known today as Iraklion. The structure and the way of improvising in play-acting lead us to believe that the speeches were derived from the union of the Venetian Komentia Del' Arte and the Cretan theatre. In this manner, a significant theatrical tradition developed in conjunction with these speeches, theatres were built and ancient drama plays, Cretan theatre and modern Zakynthian theatrical playwrights were staged.

Let us not forget however that **music** and **songs** also influenced cultural life of the Zakynthians. The dialect

found on the islands of the Ionian Sea was "married" to music and thus the famous Zakynthian ballads and serenades were born, metrical speech accompanied by the mantolinata and the small stringed orchestras. Another musical creation of Zakynthos is the **"arekies"** – a quartet populist song. This traditional form created by local inspiration has the singularity of the third voice – the "tertsas".

Another Zakynthian love is opera and light opera that unite the aristocracy with the people. Finally, melodrama also flourished on Zakynthos and operettas (romantic comedy) were presented for the first time in Greece. In 1815 the first School of Music opened on Zakynthos and a year later the Philharmonic Band was formed, which is considered to be one of the oldest in Greece.

FINE ARTS (BEAUX ARTS)

The Arts that developed and flourished on Zakynthos very early in time included **painting** and **hagiographies, silver** and **wood sculptures** and **carvings.** Significant hagiographers lived and created their works on the island while an important role in the formulation of the style was played by the Cretan artists who arrived on Zakynthos after the destruction of Handaka, around the middle of the 17th C. Among them were **Michail Damaskinos, Dimitrios** and **Georgios Moschos,**

Works of renowned Greek and foreign artists exhibited in the Museum on Zakynthos

Manolis and **Constantinos Tzannes** and **Stephanos Tzangarolas.** The works of these artists have been preserved in many churches and are also found in the Museum for Post-Byzantine Art on Zakynthos. The main characteristic of Zakynthian art is naturalism, with influences from the Italian Renaissance which –in conjunction with Byzantine art- created the **Eptanisian (Ionian) School.** During the 17th and 18th C. the Eptanisian School was limited to hagiography and the depiction of religious subjects up to the end of the 18th C. and the beginning of the 19th C., when it turned to more cosmic subjects. Among the more significant representatives of the

Eptanisian School are **Panagiotis Doxaras, Nikolaos Koutouzis, Nikolaos Kantounis,** etc.

Other than the significant hagiographical works found in the churches on Zakynthos, there are also exquisite samples of sculptures in silver, stone and wood. Many of the belfries also constitute exceptional samples of the outstanding artistry of their creators.

The entrance to the Monastery of the Virgin Mary of Skopiotissa The Church of Agia Paraskevi in Volimes

The statue of Doxa (=Glory) in Solomos Square

Folklore

If you study the customs, religions and festivals you can bring to mind the mosaic of the life and evolution of a race. Zakynthos is an island with strong religious character and faith in God. The relationship of the people with God is also significant, which even today has remained a daily and continuous association.

There are many **Christian festivals** that remained untouched by the passing

Celebrating Easter in the town of Zakynthos

of time, with their pinnacle being the services that magnetise with their rituality and solemnity the many locals and foreigners that gather on Zakynthos every year so as to be present at these significant events.

The sacred relics of Agios (=Saint) Dionysios –the patron saint of Zakynthos– predominate over the town and the rest of the island. He is celebrated twice a year, his Assumption on December 17th and the transportation of his relics from Strofades to Zakynthos on August 24th. Other than these festivals there are also quite a few others that are celebrated with especial splendidness on Zakynthos. The **Zakynthian Easter** is also celebrated with much grandeur and is characterised by its unique festivity rituals during the Holy Week before Easter. One of the more soul-stirring moments occurs when the Epitaph is carried around the town of Zakynthos, accompanied by the Philharmonic Band which plays funereal music. On Good Friday the people drink vinegar and the women throw ceramic pitchers from their windows in remembrance of the Holy Passions. The procession of this unique Epitaph –which "comes out" into the town– does not occur on the after-

noon of Good Friday, as is the case in most places in Greece, but rather early at dawn on Holy Saturday. At sunrise the procession with the Epitaph returns to the church and the bells of all the churches in the town ring out harmoniously the first Resurrection, or as the Zakynthians call it, **"the Gloria of the Crucified".** The priests change their black attire to their festival red vestments and the band fills the night with joyful paeans.

Other than the customs and religious festivals, on Zakynthos we will also come across the "antetia", which is a purely Zakynthian custom, a total of customs and habits that are devoutly maintained by the faithful. The

Through the passing eras Zakynthos maintains its cultural heritage and its local character

"anteti" takes place for "goodness" and there is always in the minds of the "antetadoron" an intimate fear that something bad will occur if it is not maintained.

It is characteristic that the Zakynthians maintained their **"antetia"** even among the ruins caused by the earthquake of 1953 when the whole of Zakynthos was destroyed.

At the **fairs and festivals** we will have the opportunity to see the **traditional dances** of Zakynthos. In addition, we can also see and admire the impressive Zakynthian costumes at the traditional festivities that take place quite a few times during the year.

The Town and its Surrounding Suburbia

Strata Marina – the most vibrant street in the town

The town of Zakynthos spreads out lengthwise between the hills of the Kastro and the Exintaveloni for approximately 2.5 km. It is a relatively narrow town with its width being defined by the formation of the land, and thus at some parts it reaches 100 m while along the length of the Ag. Haralambos River it extends to around 850 m. The façade of the enchanting town of Zakynthos spreads lengthwise along the harbour and the coastal road, the old **Strata Marina.** Two-storied and three-storied buildings with arches, restaurants, tourist shops and hotels all welcome us. At the southern corner of the town our eyes are attracted to the tall belfry and the **Church of Ag. Dionysios**, the Patron Saint of the island, which stands out among the tall trees of the suburb of Ammos. The new **Ecclesiastical Museum–Sacrarium** of the Monastery of Strofades and Ag. Dionisiou Zakynthou is housed in the ground floor of the new annex of the monastery. Among the valuable items that are exhibited here, the ones that stand out are the icons of the Virgin Mary of Thalassomachousas (13th C.) and the Virgin Mary of Pantocharas (15th C.), silver ecclesiastical items, manuscripts, documents, rare editions of ecclesiastical books and a rich collection of sacerdotal vestments.

The Church of Ag. Dionysios is one of the few buildings in the town that was not destroyed by the earthquake in 1953. This three-aisled basilica church was built in 1925 in accordance with plans by Professor Orlando.

The Patron Saint of the island

The Church of Agios Dionysios – the Patron Saint of the island

Agios Dionysios, who lived during the end of the 16th C. and the beginning of the 17th C., was a descendent of a noble family of the island – the Sigourou family. He passed the initial period of his monastic life at the Monastery of Strofades. Later, on his way to the Holy Lands he arrived in Athens where he was ordained Bishop of Aiginis. When he later fell ill and wanted to return to his monastic life, he resigned as Bishop and passed the remainder of his life at the Monastery of Anafonitrias on Zakynthos. Ag. Dionysios passed away on December 17th 1624 on Strofades, where he was buried. His relics were moved to Zakynthos almost 100 years later, on 24th August 1716. The whole of Zakynthos celebrates these two dates in memory of its Patron Saint through impressive litanies and festivals that attract thousands of the faithful.

The attractive Square of Agios Markos

Externally the belfry –which is similar to that of St. Marcus in Venice– stands out. Inside the church, the **holy tabernacle** by G. and D. Balafa is kept inside a silver etched shrine. Splendid frescos by Koutouzi and Doxara decorate the church, depicting scenes from the life of the saint. Other noteworthy works are the representation of the litany in the women's section and the wood-carved iconostasis.

Another significant church in the town is that of **Faneromenis** which dates back to the 15th C. and is situated behind the Church of Ag. Dionisios. Even though the church suffered significant damage during the earthquake in 1953, the church and its tower-like belfry were restored. In previous years, when the island still had "nobles" and "popolari", the square in front of the church was the populist's or peoples square of the town, in contrast to that of Ag. Markos Square, where the nobility congregated.

One of the old suburbs used to be situated where we are now, that of **Ammos,** a beach that has been banked up. The trees of Ammos or as they are known, the "trees of the Saint", can be found in the small square, together with the statue of the notable Zakynthian man of letters, Gr. Xenopoulos. Today there is a small park situated where his house used to be.

We continue along the coastal road called Lomberdou. The streets behind the coastal road present a different, more daily picture. Besides, the majority of the houses have been built after the 1953 earthquake that flattened the old town, leaving just a few buildings standing, which have of course altered the image of the town and

the characteristic Zakynthian architecture. The only element of the town that has remained unchanged –as it was before the earthquake– is its land planning which spreads out between the two hills, and thus preserves its old form. In addition, many recent works that have been carried out in the town, such as the unification of Solomos and Ag. Markos Squares, renovation of the façades of the buildings and infrastructure works throughout the island have recreated the enchanting image of Zakynthos, which combines the nobleness of

Solomos Square

the past with the functionability of the present.

Solomos Square dominates the town and is the largest on Zakynthos. The site where this large square is now situated used to be covered with sea-water, and which has gradually been banked up in order to cover the expansion needs of the town. The tradi-tional buildings that sur-round it house mainly the public services and museums. In the centre of the square stands out the statue of our national poet, Dionisios Solomos, while the Neo-Classical building

Panoramic view of the town that was built after the earthquake and which has arches along its façade, houses the **Public Library**, the **Cultural Centre** and the Foskolos Cinema. The history of the

Library is deeply rooted to the past, as is the history of the civilization and art on the island.

The town of Zakynthos after sunset

The first library on Zakynthos was opened in 1628 and was housed in the Kastro which then surrounded the town. During the years of the Ionian State an official library was formed which was unified in 1935 with the Foskolian Library, which had been established in 1888. The large earthquake in 1953 and the subsequent fire completely destroyed 33,000 volumes, including the autographs of Kolokotroni and Lord Byron, which were valuable records of Zakynthian history. The library was established again from scratch with the contributions of notable Zakynthian patrons of the arts and letters and today it has more than 60,000 books, including some rare books relating to the history and folklore of Zakynthos. **The Museum of Occupation and National Resistance** can be found on the ground floor, with exhibits from the recent Italian-German Occupation period, as well as older occupation periods by the conquerors of the island.

On the north-eastern side of the square (near the sea) we have the Chapel of **Ag. Nikolaos of Molou,** built in

The pretty Church of Agios Nikolaos of Molos

1561 by the sailors' guild. This church is the only Venetian building that survived the earthquake and subsequent fire. It has been restored externally and lined with stone from the quarry at Geraka.

The **Museum for Post-Byzantine** Art is found on the south side of Solomos Square, which houses many notable exhibits from Ionian (Eptanesian) and Cretan art. The Museum is built on the site of the old Church of Pantokratora and many exhibits are derived from churches and monasteries that were destroyed from the earthquake of 1953. Entering the Museum, in the hall on the right side of the ground floor we can see two majestic Post-Byzantine iconostases masterpieces from the Churches of Ag. Dimitrios of Kolla (1690) and Pantokratora (1621). In the halls on the ground floor we also have the opportunity to admire various works of Cretan and Eptanesian artists from the 16th and 17th Centuries, of mainly Byzantine style with traces of Italian Renaissance and Flemish artistry. In the hall on the left side of the ground floor we have the impressive mock-up model of the pre-earthquake town of Zakynthos constructed by G. Manesis. Frescos from the Church of Ag. Andreas of Volimon comprise the main exhibits in the hall on the first floor.

A stroll up the paved street that joins Solomos Square with Ag. Markos Square comprises a pleasant and graphic walkabout. The triangular square with its significant historical memories is one of the more graphic places in the town. Here in 1797 –the period of the French Democrats– the popolari burned the **Libro d'Oro** and symbolically planted the Tree of Freedom. In the square we have the austere **Catholic Church of Ag. Markos,** founded in 1518. The hands of the old clock of the forou, which has been standing next to the Catholic Church since 1807, counts the passing time.

At the beginning of the 1800's, at the site where the Solomos and Eminent **Zakynthians Museum** is situated next to the Catholic Church of Ag. Markos, was one of the most significant churches of the town –the Church of Pantokrator– which was destroyed by the last earthquake. When we now enter the Museum we are greeted by the statue of Dionysios

The statue of Dionysios Solomos

The iconostasis of the church –
An exhibit from the Museum of
Byzantine and Post-Byzantine Art

Solomos, sculptured by G. Vroutsou. On entering, we pause at the piece of the tree trunk which then grew on Strani hill and under whose shade Solomos wrote some of his renowned works, including the "Hymn of Freedom"– our National Anthem. The museum was recently renovated, its works of art and archives preserved and restored by experts, and the art gallery was modified from the beginning in accordance with museumology guidelines. Finally, among the paintings, folkloric exhibits, historical documents, traditional costumes and other items that are exhibited at the Museum, that which stands out is the Mausoleum of Andreas Kalvos and Dionysios Solomos.

A piece of the tree whose shade inspired Dionysios Solomos

Leaving Solomos Museum behind us, we continue along the recently paved commercial street of the town –**21st May Street**– which then changes its name to **Alexandros Roma.** Many commercial shops can be found under the traditional arches. **Argasari Street,** situated behind the Courthouse, ends up at the **Palia Vrisi** (=Old Tap). From here the road leading to the **Church of Pikridiotissa** begins, and from here an old path leads to the Kastro at the top of **Bochali hill.**

Next to the church we can see the marble slat that informs us that it was here that Kolokotroni –while looking at the mountains of enslaved Greece– decided to lead the revolution.

The Temple of Analipseos, a three-aisled basilica 16th C. church with a tower-like belfry is situated in the same area as the house where the Greco-Italian poet, Nikolaos Oungos Foskolos, lived. This site is now a garden that includes a wonderful statue of a reclining angel by the Zakynthian sculpture Vitsari. At the opposite corner is a small chapel with a lit oil lamp. A sign informs us that Nikos Foskolos used to read with the light from this candle when he was a child.

The Catholic Church of Agios Markos

At the end of Roma Street we meet **Ag. Pavlos Square.**

The church of the same name was completely destroyed by the earthquake, as were the majority of the churches in the town. From this square the road splits into two: one leading to Volimes and the other to Laganas and the Airport. On **Lazarou Street** we have the homonymous church dating back to around 1500, which initially functioned as a monastery. Small notable icons decorate the interior of the church, including that of the Virgin Mary of Vrefokratousas, which is carried in a procession around the streets of the town on the night of Easter Sunday.

Returning back to the north side of the town, we pass through Solomos Square and take the coastal road leading to the suburbs of **Kryoneri** and Tsilivi. The name of

the street changes to Dionisiou Roma. Here inside the small narrow streets of the town we come across the small **Chapel of the Kyrias of Angelon**, built in 1687. A small distance away is the Metropolitan **Church of Ag. Nikolaos of Xenon**, which has been erected on the site of the old church that had been destroyed by

The Larnaka of Agios Dionysios

the earthquake. The church took its name from the custom to bury foreigners to the town in the yard.

Continuing along the coastal road we pass by the EOT beach (=National Tourist Board) and the **Church of Ag. Triada** with its tower-like tall belfry. This church was built recently and has been adorned with the wood-carved iconostasis and the old icon of the Virgin Mary of Laourentenas that were brought from the Church of Ag. Triada that was situated in the Kastro. Behind the church is the English Cemetery founded in 1675 in order to bury the British inhabitants of Zakynthos. Above the graves we can admire masterpieces of marble monuments by Geraka that are similar to temples. This region is known by the locals as the **English Monuments.**

A natural continuation is the suburb of **Kryoneri,** which takes its name from the Venetian tap on the other side

KEY TO MAP

- Hospital
- Bus Station
- Church – Monastery
- Beach
- Water sports
- Ferry Line

- Pharmacy
- Port – Marina
- Taxi
- Bank
- Post Office
- OTE – Telephone
- Fuel Station

ΠΑΡΘΕΝΟΥ ΜΑΡΙΑΣ ΧΡΥΣΟΠΗΓΗΣ
VIRGIN MARY OF CHRISSOPIGI

ΚΑΣΤΡΟ
CASTLE

ΝΟΣΟΚΟΜΕΙΟ
HOSPITAL

ΜΗΤΡΟΠΟΛΗ
METROPOLIS

ΛΙΜΕΝΑΡΧΕΙΟ
PORT AUTHORITY

KILINI
ΚΥΛΛΗΝΗ

TO BOCHALI
TO TRAGAKI
TO GERAKARI

TO TSILIVI
TO PANOS

TO KALAMAKI
TO ARGASSI
TO VASSILIKOS
TO PORTO ROMA

TO AIRPORT
TO LAGANAS
TO MARATHIA

of the road. This tap is portrayed in the novel "Kokkinos Vrachos" (=Red Rock) by the Zakynthian author Grygorios Xenopoulos.

BOCHALI – STRANI HILL

Night view of the town

Towering over the town is the green-filled **hill of Bochali** and the Venetian Kastro from the Middle-Ages. Before reaching the crest of the hill we take a break at the **Church of Ag. Georgios** of Filikon, where those being initiated into the Friendly Society gave their vows of allegiance (a depiction of this ceremony can be seen in the **Post-Byzantine Museum**), who included many well-known heroes of the Revolution. Inside this small temple and to the right of the icon-ostasis is a list of the names of those fighters who pledged their allegiance here.

We will make one more stop at the **Eptanesian Naval Museum,** a new museum that links the historical course of Greece –especially that of the Ionian Islands– with shipping. The Naval Museum contains mainly pictures with maritime content, surrounded by relevant objects and items that form a collection which gives us the opportunity to learn about the maritime evolution of our country. The Museum is divided into seven thematic units, from the time of Antiquity up to the modern age.

Bochali, famous for its flowers and crafts, is mentioned in the texts of Kastrinian "nodaron" (=notaries) from the beginning of the 16th C. A characteristic reference to Bochali at that time was the arched and vaulted windmills that existed from the initial years of the Venetian Occupation period up to the English Occupation period.

It is thought that at the north-western corner of this Middle-Aged Zakynthian suburb, in the area of Aringos or Antilalos, a stadium of ancient Zakynthos was possibly situated. In the 18th C. a statue depicting Apollo, Artemis and Aphrodite was found here, and this statue is now exhibited in the Tiepolo Museum in Venice.

The entrance to the Venetian Kastro and the Lion of Agios Markos

The **Church of the Virgin Mary of Chrisopigi** is situated in Bochali Square. Its interior is dominated by the gold-plated, wood-carved iconostasis and the old icon of the Virgin Mary, which historians maintain has inscribed in

Byzantine numbers the date 848 and the signature of the Byzantine hagiographer Panisalkos.

The road from Bochali continues uphill, leading to the Venetian Kastro, with fortifications that are strongly reminiscent of similar defensive works in many regions in Greece. Passing through the three successive gates in order to enter the area where ancient Zakynthos was built, we can discern on the third gate **the Lion of Ag. Markos**, the symbol of the Venetians.

The remains of an enchanting period

Among the tall pine trees are the ruins of old houses and reputable churches that gave life to the Kastro. However, today only the dungeons and the gunpowder storerooms with their barred windows remain standing. Reaching the highest part of the Kastro, we find ourselves in the area where Psofida was probably sited. During one of the large earthquakes that changed the morphology of the region, the Kastro was cut off from the adjacent hill, that of **Exintaveloni**. Thus that which the besiegers to the island could not achieve over many years was finally accomplished by a natural phenomenon – the complete destruction of the cyclopean walls of the ancient capital.

After visiting the Kastro and Bochali, we pass through the main road and reach **Strani hill.** Following the paved trail we arrive at an open, flat place from which we can see the whole island and the mainland opposite. From

here our national poet, Dionysios Solomos, watched the progress of the besiegement of Mesolongi and inspired, penned the wonderful poem "Eleftheri Poliorkimeni" (= Liberated Besieged) and the "Hymn for Freedom". The verses of this poem were set to music by the Corfiote composer, Nikolaos Mantzaros, and are now the National Anthem of Greece.

The statue of Dionysios Solomos situated on Strani Hill

50-51: The town of Zakynthos

Zakynthos - Argasi Vasilikos - Gerakas Strofadia

1st EXCURSION

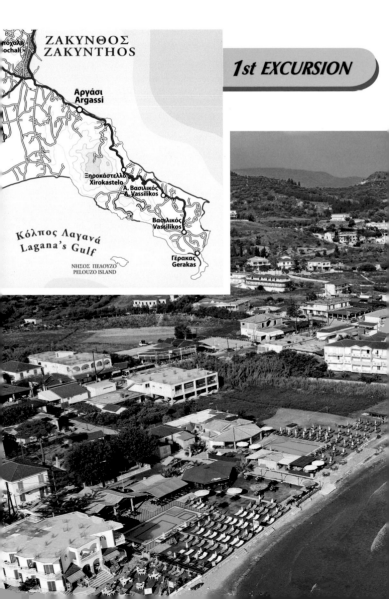

The first excursion that we recommend basically covers the promontory at Geraka, the south-eastern part of Zakynthos. This is a short but exceptionally beautiful route which gives us the opportunity to enjoy a swim at some of the best beaches on Zakynthos, while at the same time exploring this enchanting part of the island.

On leaving the town we turn left at the small bridge on the **River of Ag. Haralambi,** and come across the church of the same name, built in 1729, which was an offering by the local inhabitants to Ag. Haralambos, who had saved the island from a plague epidemic. The church has been characterized an archaeological

Beautiful Argasi

The old small stone bridge at Argasi

monument and it is worth stopping to admire the outside adornment of the church, the gold-etched, wood-carved iconostasis and the small old icons.

Continuing on our journey, just before the old suburb of **Argasi** we come across an old manorial house to our right, which during the period when the Friendly Society was formed, was used as a meeting place by its members.

Today Argasi is a tourist suburb of Zakynthos, which -due to its continual development- has almost united with the town. The beach is on the one side of the road while the other side is shaded by **Skopo,** a low but interesting hill for explorers. At its peak is the white **Chapel of the Virgin Mary of Skopiotissa** that was erected in 1624 on the site of the old Sanctuary of Artemidas. The church, which is the only one on Zakynthos with a cupola, has the form of a free cross and its interior is adorned with notable frescoes. The iconostasis stands out, built of stone in contrast to the wooden-carved iconostasis found in other church-es on Zakynthos.

It is said that when the weather is clear, this church can be seen throughout Zakynthos. Coming down the path we pause once again to enjoy the view from **Belvedere Hill** (beautiful view), as the Venetians called Skopo.

Continuing along the main road we see the remnants of an old bridge with arches that is situated on the beach, built around 1885. After leaving Argasi the road winds uphill and the beach spreads out below us. From above we can discern the huts made of dry grass that were built by the locals to protect themselves from the sun.

After Argasi we come across a signpost informing us that we are entering **Vasilikos,** which comprises a number of small settlements that had developed gradually. According to an old tradition, the locals who fished along the beach of Agios Nikolaos when there were calm waters could clearly see the marble steps of the grand palace of King Zakynthos. They also maintain that columns, pillars and amphoras are buried in the shallow waters, as well as a huge male

The graphical Chapel of the Virgin Mary of Skopiotissa

statue. The narrations and the secretive manner of the people state that they had truly seen what they alleged, which is also partially confirmed by research work carried out by archaeologists, who consider Vasilikos to be a possible site for the ancient palace of Zakynthos. And from this hypothesis the region has taken its name.

It is worth making a short detour to visit the **Folkloric Museum in Namoroza,** a new village that hosts many folkloric exhibits and items of historical interest.

About 1 km after **Xilokastelo** we meet on our right a dirt road leading to the beaches of **Sekania** and **Dafni.** Both Sekania and Dafni are beaches rich in sand and are among the more significant biotopes for the reproduction of the **Caretta-Caretta turtles.** There are measures in effect at these beaches, as well as at most of the beaches along Laganas Bay, for the protection of the sea-turtles. The road to **Vasilikos** continues through the pine forest, which cools us and relaxes us. Even the bends in the road become softer and "nonchalant" as we proceed.

Various crossroads trial off the main road, leading to the beautiful beaches in the region. **Porto Zoro** is the first beach that we meet, with sand and a few tavernas on the sea.

Just after Porto Zoro is the first exit to **Banana Beach.** This beach, with its shallow waters and width that reaches dozens of meters, is considered to be one of the best beaches on Zakynthos. Slender white waterlilies have sprouted among the sand, giving the beach a tropical look. A short distance away is the equally attractive **beach of Ag. Nikolaos.** To the right of the beach is the Chapel of Ag. Nikolaos which after the 1984 earthquake was moved from its old site on the hill to the rocks. The right side of the beach is narrower and has therefore less people, and this attracts those sunbathers who want to enjoy their swimming in a more serene atmosphere.

The road that we have travelled so far branches out

The nest and the little turtle that is battling for its survival

The National Sea-Park on Zakynthos

The National Sea-Park on Zakynthos is situated in the southern part of the island. The greater part of the Park includes the land and sea regions of the Gulf of Laganas where the more significant egg-laying beaches of the Caretta-Caretta sea-turtles can be found in the Mediterranean. The egg-laying period for the turtles lasts from June to August. The female turtles come out onto the beach at night, dig their nests to a depth of about 50 cm and lay their eggs here. After about 60 days the little turtles make their first journey to the sea, usually during the night. As is underlined in the informational brochures handed out by the Society for the Protection of the Caretta-Caretta Sea-Turtle, it is necessary for them to find their way without the intervention of man, since scientists believe that the first trip that they take is the most decisive one. Members of the Society have installed signs on the beaches where the eggs hatch that inform us as to the ways of protecting the egg-laying of the Caretta-Caretta. We are not allowed to remain on the beaches where the turtles hatch after sunset and before sunrise. Beach chairs and umbrellas are also prohibited from these sandy beaches, except within specific areas. The area of the Sea-Park is representative of Mediterranean and island ecosystems. The coastal zone includes sandy beaches, wetlands and rocky shores, while the land is characterised by forest and scattered agricultural areas.

For more information you can visit the offices of the Park in Argasi or go to their website at:
www.nmp-zak.org.

Sandy Banana beach

The enchanting beaches of Porto Zoro and Porto Roma

towards the direction of Porto Roma and the beach at Geraka. The left branch takes us to the beaches at **Mavratzi** and **Porto Roma,** which took its name from the renowned Zakynthian, Alexandro Roma, who had his home in the region. The dirt road to Mavratzi ends up at another sandy beach with crystal blue waters.

The beach at **Geraka,** at the end of the promontory of the same name, is one of the most impressive on the island. The whole beach, as well as the red vertical rocks at the promontory that surround it, is an impressive sight from the top of the path. The fine sand and the shallow sky-blue waters complement this enchanting scene.

Gerakas, as with the other beaches in southern Zakynthos, is an egglaying site for the protected Caretta-Caretta sea-turtle. The local inhabitants, as well as foreign visitors, feel it is their duty to protect the egg-laying sites of these turtles which are in danger of becoming extinct in the Mediterranean. In many places on the beach we see small wire fences – that look like an upside down basket-protecting small patches of sand. Nests have been located under these fences, which are protected and observed by

scientists and members of the Society for the Protection of the Caretta-Caretta.

The impressive rock at the promontory rises along the left side of Geraka Beach. From the crest of the promontory we can see the outer beach of Geraka which we can reach only by caique. Opposite the beach is the private **islet of Pelouzo**, where we can discern the ruins of the monastery that stood there once upon a time.

Swimming with no cares in the blue waters of Gerakas

The Strofades Islets

The **Strofades** Islets or Strofadia, also known as the "floating islands" due to their lowlands that do not exceed 10 m in height, are situated 37 n.m. south of Zakynthos. During the summer we can visit the island daily by caique from the town or from Laganas. There are two islets: Arpina and Stamvranio.

During the 13th C. Eirini, the wife of Byzantine Emperor Laskareos, built a monastery on Arpina –the larger of the two islets and the one that is inhabited– dedicated to the Metamorphosis of Sotiros and the Theotoko of Pantochara. The homonymous church that is adorned by a marble iconostasis and many old icons is situated on the first floor of the tower. Many holy monks lived in the monastery, including Ag. Dionysios, who later gave his name to it. In 1440 the monastery took its current form as a fortress-monastery after repair-work was carried out by Emperor Ioannis Paleologos. The islet was raided at various times by pirates and barbarians, which resulted in the transfer of the holy relics of Ag. Dionysios to Zakynthos for safekeeping. The now empty grave of the saint is situated in the **Temple of Ag. Georgios** on the ground floor of the monastery's tower. The tower rises majestically before the monastery to a height of 26 m.

The blue-green waters at the beach of Agios Nikolaos

Zakynthos – Kalamaki Laganas – Agalas – Keri Limni Keriou

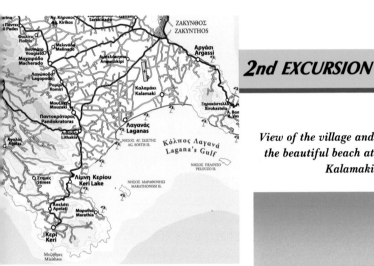

2nd EXCURSION

View of the village and the beautiful beach at Kalamaki

We continue to explore Zakynthos with our second excursion where we will visit the very touristic areas of Kalamaki and Laganas, as well as the unique fascination of the promontory of Keri and its coastal region, that of Limni.

68-69:
Laganas – a variety of choices in this wonderful tourist resort

After leaving the town behind us, the first village that we meet is tourist-orientated Kalamaki, about 8 km from the centre of Zakynthos. The fascinating

The small Islet of Agios Sostis – A graphic "brush-stroke" in Laganas

beach in this region attracts hundreds of visitors every day who enjoy their swimming and their sun-bathing along this sandy beach, with its high rocks on the edge and the foamy waves breaking on them. On top of the beach is a large piece of land covered with sand-dunes, or as the Zakynthians call them, "ammokoulou-mous". During Spring sea-lilies sprout in the sand and it is said that the wind transfers their aroma deep into the sea. There are imposing rocks on the left side of the beach made of gypsum, the so-called **Gypsolithi** or Ipsolithi.

To continue our visit of the southern beaches of Zakynthos, we have to again go inland, passing close by the island's airport in the area of **Ambelokipi** and after following the signposts, we reach **Laganas.** This is probably the most tourist-orientated region on Zakynthos, with many Greek and foreign restaurants, bars, tourist shops and large and smaller hotel complexes. At the end of the road we stand before the

spread-out moorage at Laganas, with a coastal length of more than 9 km, which classifies it among the largest beaches in Greece. Its shallow and deep waters are perfect for water-games and water-sports and relaxation in the fine light-coloured sand. It seems that the turtles have

made their quality choices since the beaches where they frequent are the best on the island!

Along the right edge of the moorage and just a few meters from the shore is the microscopic **islet of Ag. Sosti.,** which took its name from the church that is situated there. This islet was joined to the mainland up until 1633 when it was separated by an earthquake,

Swimming and relaxing at Laganas beach

Intense night-life in Laganas

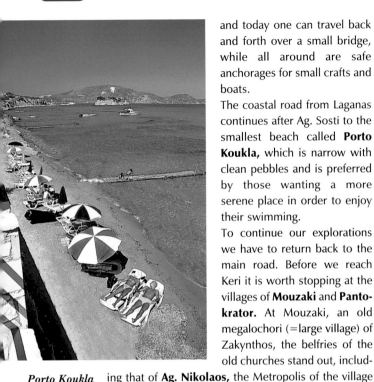

Porto Koukla Beach

The region of Myzithres constitutes an especially natural beauty spot on the island

and today one can travel back and forth over a small bridge, while all around are safe anchorages for small crafts and boats.

The coastal road from Laganas continues after Ag. Sosti to the smallest beach called **Porto Koukla,** which is narrow with clean pebbles and is preferred by those wanting a more serene place in order to enjoy their swimming.

To continue our explorations we have to return back to the main road. Before we reach Keri it is worth stopping at the villages of **Mouzaki** and **Pantokrator.** At Mouzaki, an old megalochori (=large village) of Zakynthos, the belfries of the old churches stand out, including that of **Ag. Nikolaos,** the Metropolis of the village which was built in 1815 but was recently restored. Just a little further down is the **Church of the Virgin Mary**, which has the date 1741 engraved on its iconostasis. Approaching Pantokratora, we can see among the trees the **Sarakinas mansion.** This was a deserted stately characteristic example of a Zakynthian country-house which –despite the wear and tear of time– still maintains its grandeur, giving us a sense of the old prosperous period of Zakynthos. Arriving in Pantokratora we meet the old **Church of Sotira** or Pantokratora, built on the top of the hill. This church has elements of Byzantine architecture with the two-headed eagle –the Byzantine emblem– standing out on the floor of the temple. It is said that the temple was built by Empress Poulcheria during her visit to Zakynthos.

Another traditional Zakynthian village that we must

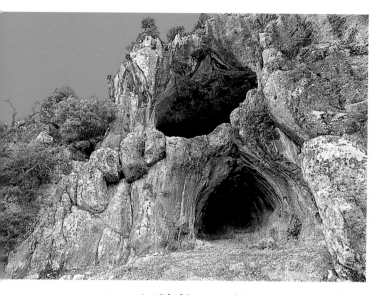

stop at is **Lithakia,** one of the kefalochoria (=larger villages) of Zakynthos, where earthquakes and desertion have left their mark. The main church of the village, **Faneromeni,** is dedicated to the Virgin Mary and

was built during the 14th C. Inside the church we can see icons from various churches in the region that have been destroyed. Just outside the village are the scattered remnants of **Paleokastrou,** one of the few archaeological sites that we can see on Zakynthos. Other than these old ruins, we can also see part of the **Venetian tower** that is still standing in the region.

Between Lithakia and **Agalas** is an abrupt gorge, the so-called **Abyss** that was formed by the earthquakes in 1633. At the bottom of the gorge is a small spring with drinkable water that is quite

digestible. The water gathers into a small pool and terminates at the Kornou stream, which opens into the sea. Situated on the hill above the pool is the Human Cave –as it is called by the locals– which was the gravesite for 150 people when pirates torched the cave.

Agalas is situated between the foot of the hill and the western shores of Zakynthos, surrounded by pine trees. We turn right, following the signposts for **Damianos' Cave.** Following the path that becomes better paved after a certain point we finally reach the two-storied Cave, which Nature decorated with impressive stalactites and stalagmites. Just outside the village we can see 15th C. wells nestling among the age-old olive trees that are used to water them. These

Damianos Cave, the Sarakina Mansion and the Church of Faneromeni are sites in the region that are worth seeing

wells have been built in accordance with traditional Zakynthian architecture. The region takes its name from these wells and is known as **Dodeka Pigadia** (=Twelve Wells).

On the south-western shores of Zakynthos is the Cape of **Marathias.** The Church of the **Virgin Mary of Keriotissas** is situated in the flat area below the village of Keri, the place where her icon was discovered. The locals say that all attempts to move the icon have failed since it always returns back during the night. Old-timers narrate the miracle performed by the icon when fog covered the village in the middle of summer and thus protected its inhabitants from the fury of the pirates that plagued the island.

A road with some bends ends up at a path that leads us to **Faro,** where if the sky is clear we can admire one of the famous June sunsets. The Ionian Sea with its transparent waters spreads out before us, with the rocks at Marathia on the one side and the abrupt continuation of the hill on the other side blending harmoniously into the scenery, and thus creating an impres-

The late afternoon in picturesque Keri is a kaleidoscope of colours

The large arch in Marathia is a monument of Nature

sive picture. As we leave, another imposing picture captures us, that of the vertical rocks that are sprayed by the green and blue waters of the Ionian Sea – the so-called **Mikri and Megali Myzithra.**

Just before entering the **Lake at Keri,** which is a natural harbour in southern Zakynthos, we cross the road that leads to where the now destroyed Middle-Ages Keri used to be. The tar springs that were known way back in Antiquity are found in Keri. At the entrance to the village is **"Herodotus' Pigi"**, with water that gushes out of the

The caves at Keri

80-81: The blue waters of Keri Lake that reflect Nature's greenery

ground. At the bottom we can still discern the tar that the locals used in previous years to calk their ships.

From the shore of the lake little boats depart to visit the sea-caves, the spectacular pieces of white rock, Mikri and Megali Myzithra, pass by Marathia with the imposing stone arches of the rocks and terminate at **Marathonisi.** Here, when it's not blowing, we can enjoy a swim in the warm clear waters that even the sea-turtles prefer for swimming around!

Marathia and Marathonisi

Zakynthos – Macherado Lagopodo – Kiliomenos Ag. Leon – Maries Porto Vromi – Navagio Anafonitria

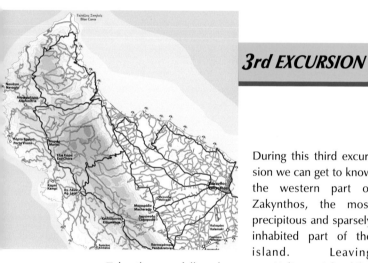

3rd EXCURSION

During this third excursion we can get to know the western part of Zakynthos, the most precipitous and sparsely inhabited part of the island. Leaving Zakynthos, we follow the route to Volimes. A few kilometres later we reach the cross-road for Macherado, and we turn here to visit the village. The road passes through the Zakynthian plain, fertile lands where raisins are cultivated, together with various vegetable plots.

We soon reach **Macherado,** which is the second largest village –after Katastari– in the plain. At the entrance to the village the high belfry of Ag. Mavra stands out among the cypress trees, constructed in the form of a tower. The **Church of Ag. Mavra** is the second most significant church on the island and it is said that when its bells peal out, they can be heard almost throughout the island. In accordance with tradition, the icon of Ag.

The Church of Agia Mavra and its renowned belfry

The tower-like belfry of Agios Nikolaos

Mavras was discovered by a shepherd from the village of Lagopodo, hanging on a fence. He unsuccessful tried three times to take it back to his village, but each time the icon miraculously returned during the night back to the place where it was first discovered. In this manner the icon showed where it wanted its church to be built. The church with its imposing tower-like Venetian belfry has few adornments externally, but inside it is especially striking with its gold-plated carved iconostasis and its artistic frescoes dominating the main sanctuary. The women's section is carved in wood with many carvings reminiscent of eastern works of art. The church celebrates on May 3rd, that of Ag. Mavras and Ag. Timotheos and the services continue throughout the night. The faithful arrive in their thousands not only from Zakynthos but also from other parts of Greece. The second church in the village, which was recently restored, is that of **Ypapanti,** dating back to the 14th C., and is adorned externally with remarkable carvings. Its stone belfry is among the tallest on the island.

A panoramic view of the Monastery of Eleftherotria and the iconostasis from the Monastery of Yperagathos

Entering the suburb of **Melinado,** we find that its houses have joined those of Macherado. Remnants from the Church of Ag. Dimitrios have been found here, including marble columns and a slab with an inscription in the Doric dialect that is derived from the ancient Temple of Opitaidas Artemidos. In the adjacent village of **Vougiato** we come across the **Church of the Virgin Mary.** Following the road behind the church we reach the **Church of Ag. Ioannis Theologos,** which was possibly built on the ruins of the Church of Opitaidas Artemidos.

Continuing on our way to the village of **Lagopodo,** we see from afar the women's **Monastery of the Virgin Mary of Eleftherotrias,** which even though was built recently (1961), the ashlar masonry that was used gives it a weathered and aged appearance. The monastery that is reminiscent of a fortress has a wonderful view of the Skopo and the Kastro in the town. At the village we can take a break to visit the **Church of Sotiros** and then continue on our way to **Kiliomeno.**

The original name of the village was Ag. Nikolaos from the name of the old church that was situated in its centre and it has been renovated externally. The shrine, which was recently gilded is also impressive with its wood-carved iconostasis, where deep red and cypress green dominate among its hagiographies and adornments. Opposite us is the remarkable **tower-like belfry of Ag. Nikolaos** which was built in 1893, in accordance with the date etched on its steps. The adornments of the church are unique, divided into floor levels with circular windows and balconies in the style of the belfry.

Before leaving the village, we should detour to the **Monastery of the Virgin Mary of Yperagathou,** built on the slope of the hill near the peak of **Athera.** At the entrance to this small and now deserted monastery is an ashlar masonry cistern that is one of the largest on Zakynthos. Returning to the main road, we follow the signposts to **Ag. Leonta, the village** that takes its name from the main 14th C. church. Just before entering the village we come to a crossroad leading to the villages of **Loucha** and **Gyri** perched on the hills of Zakynthos. With small stone houses covered with ceramic tiles, lost in the greenery of Nature, these villages give us a different perspective of Zakynthos. The first inhabitants of this region came from Mani in the Peloponnese and so they built their houses following the architectural traditions of their homeland. Approaching Loucha, a half torn down

The villages of Kiliomeno and Kambi verify the scenicness of the island. A traditional grass hut

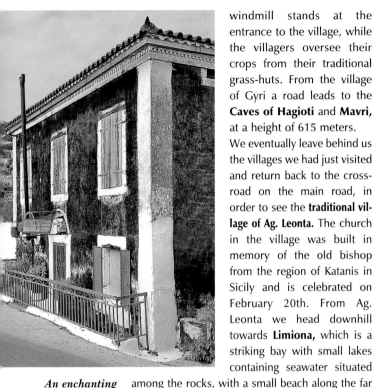

An enchanting house in Exo Chora

windmill stands at the entrance to the village, while the villagers oversee their crops from their traditional grass-huts. From the village of Gyri a road leads to the **Caves of Hagioti** and **Mavri,** at a height of 615 meters.

We eventually leave behind us the villages we had just visited and return back to the cross-road on the main road, in order to see the **traditional village of Ag. Leonta.** The church in the village was built in memory of the old bishop from the region of Katanis in Sicily and is celebrated on February 20th. From Ag. Leonta we head downhill towards **Limiona,** which is a striking bay with small lakes containing seawater situated among the rocks, with a small beach along the far side.

The day passes and if we want to complete our tour of the western shores of Zakynthos, we should start again soon. So we then continue towards the **village of Kambi**, built along the foot of the steep rocks of Schizas. At the highest point of the rock stands a large stone cross – homage to the patriots who lost their lives here during the occupation period. Climbing to the top of the rock we pass by the **Mycenean cemetery** with its ashlar masonry graves, from which however all findings have been removed.

After Kambi we turn towards Exo Chora. The parish church of the village, Ag. Nikolaos, is adorned with its iconostasis dated 1700 and

notable icons. If we like to explore, we can ask the local villagers about the road that leads to **Kato Lakko.** At this point we see an almost circular piece of land at a depth of almost 30 meters that is enclosed all round by vertical rocks. The most logical explanation for this is that some-time back in time this was a cave whose roof collapsed. The next village that we will visit has the unusual name of **Maries.** According to tradition its "god-parents" were Maria Magdalene and Maria Klopa who were the first to preach Christianity on the island. There is a 15th C. church in the village that is dedicated to Maria Magdalene, which is celebrated on June 22nd. From Maries one can reach the top of **Vrachiona** by following the even path. You will need an hour or so to reach the top but it is worth the effort since you will be able to enjoy the unique view of the western craggy shores of Zakynthos and the translucent waters of the Ionian Sea.

We are now just a hair's breath away from the most famous beach on Zakynthos and one of the most renowned in the Mediterranean. In order to reach the

Porto Vromi Bay – One of the more beautiful corners of Zakynthos

The imposing Monastery of Agios Georgios of Krimnon

beach of Ag. Georgiou –better known as **Navagio** (=Shipwreck)– we descend to the Bay of **Porto Vromi,** a small harbour from which caiques depart for Navagio many times during the day.

The trip to this famous beach is enchanting. The blue-green waters of the Ionian Sea reflect on the white lime-stone rocks while the trees grow at various places, defying the crags and adding green brush-strokes to the landscape. Entering the Bay of Ag. Georgiou we see before us the beach with its coarse white sand. The rusting shipwreck in the middle adds that extra special element to the scenery and the vertical white rocks that surround it adds a touch of wild beauty.

We continue on our trip through western Zakynthos with Maries as our starting point. We cannot end our journey without stopping at **Anafonitria** and the **Monastery of Ag. Georgios of Krimnon**, which was previously built right next to the rocks and from here it got its name. The monastery was built around 1540 by the monk Varlaam Beleti. It was here that the Patron

Saint of Cephalonia, Ag. Gerasimos, took his monastic vows. Following the path that leads to a flat piece of land below the monastery, we can see the cave where the Saint secluded himself. The monastery was also where the theologian and historian, **Pachomios Rousanos,** wrote the greater part of his work, and his grave may be seen in the courtyard of the monastery. With the passing of time, land corrosion and destructions from raids, the monastery gradually moved around until it was built on a safe site which is also where it is today. If we continue straight along the dirt-road we eventually reach the rocks above Navagio and from here we have a unique view of the majestic works of Nature.

The locals narrate a wonderful legend concerning the icon of the Virgin Mary of Anafonitrias. During the capture of Constantinople a cargo ship sailing from the Turkish city sank off Zakynthos. Local residents found the icon of the Virgin Mary of Vrefokratousas among the rocks and built a small chapel, followed later by the monastery. It is said that a blinking light was emitted from the site where it was found, as if it was shouting, and from this the monastery was given the nickname "Anafonitria". The **Monastery of the Virgin Mary Anafonitria** was build in the 15th C. and is one of eight

The unique beauty of Navagio Beach that has repeatedly been called one of the best in the world

monasteries that were not destroyed by the 1953 earthquake. On entering the monastery we see before us a tower from the Middle Ages with 6 scalders, which today is used as a belfry. The church is a three-aisled wooden roofed basilica, which are unique exceptions to Zakynthian ecclesiastical architecture, together with that of Skopiotissas.

Zakynthos – Tsilivi Planos – Alykanas – Alykes Katastari – Skoulikado Ag. Dimitrios – Ag. Kirykos Sarakinado

4th EXCURSION

During the 4th Excursion that we recommend, we will cover the more tourist-orientated north-eastern part of Zakynthos and we will return to the town via the highland villages of the plain. Two kilometres outside the town is **Akrotiri,** the region where the noblemen of the island chose to build their summerhouses, including the Solomos Family. The old Solomos summerhouse today belongs to the Chronopoulou family and has been renovated with only the stone steps leading to the orangery being a connective link to the past. The **Vodi Islets** –which in the past was linked to the mainland by a small bridge– stand out in the sea opposite the Cape.

Tsilivi is the first tourist village that we will come across

Psarrou,
One more
attractive
beach that is
worth
discovering

just a short distance from the town, only 6 km. With its extended sandy beach surrounded by greenery, this is an ideal place for your holidays. The Toraditis Cape or Gidakia protects the bay from strong winds. Above the cape we can see a Venetian "Vardiola" (old observation post) showing intense signs of the passing time. Continuing on our route along the coastal road, we reach **Plano,** another graphical village geared for tourism. Many crossroads lead off from the main road to small coves and beaches, such as **Aboula, Pachiammos, Drosia, Psarrou** ands many more that are worth exploring by yourself.

Tsilivi – A large beach with golden-coloured sand and crystal-clear shallow waters

Other than the coastal settlements we can also make small detours inland towards the villages in the plain. **Gerakaria, Ano**, **Meso** and **Kato Chorio, Tragaki** and green-filled **Kipseli** are just a few of the villages that we can visit. The villagers here are involved mainly in olive and vine cultivations, producing the well-known Zakynthian wine. We can see many orchards and olive groves in the plain. In August on both sides of the road there is a spectacular view of the dried raisins spread out under the sun, a product that in the past supported the economy of the island.

One last stop before reaching Alykes is the village of **Alykana,** situated in a region that is of especial archaeological interest. In excava-

tions carried out in Alykana, Mycenean vessels were discovered while in the region of Pyrgos archaeologists discovered a destroyed grave vault from the same period. These findings, together with some others from the surrounding area, led scientists to believe that the ancient city of Arcadia was once upon a time situated here. The beach of **Ammoudi** in Alykana is the natural continuation of the large beach at Alykes. The second beach of Alykana and the one at Ag. Kyriakis can be found at the Cape of Ag. Kyriakis, which separates the two villages. The small Skourti River passes next to the road at the entrance to **Alykes,** with an arched stone bridge that was built by the British conquerors. Behind the beach are the salt-pans that give the village its name.

After enjoying this coastal route, we can choose to return by the highland road that passes through the villages in the plain. We first meet the largest village -population wise- in Zakynthos, that of Katastari. The greater part of the island is built amphitheatrically on the side of the hill, overlooking the Bay of Alykes. The church in the village is dedicated to **Ag. Theodorous** and hosts icons, sections of iconostases and notable decorative and utilitarian objects from old neighbouring churches that no longer exist. **Katastari** is also known for its musical traditions. It has its own philharmonic band that accompanies the litanies and festivals of the village.

The next village we meet is **Pigadakia,** where we can

Alykes – A frequently visited resort centre with a variety of water sports

visit the **Vertatsio Folkloric Museum** which through its exhibits guides us through another era unknown to the majority of people. Near the Museum is the Church of Ag. Panteleimona, together with a piece of the old belfry of the temple with three bells, with the date 1611 engraved on it. Inside the church is a sulphurous curative well under the Altar. It is said that the waters of the well situated under the Altar of the Church of **Ag. Panteleimona** shake on the day the Saint celebrates and the faithful take this water home instead of the Holy

A visit to the Vertatsio Folkloric Museum with its plethora of folkloric exhibits

Water. The church was destroyed by an earthquake and only the belfry, the icon of Ag. Panteleimona and the iconostasis survived; they now adorn the current church.

From Pigadakia we can either follow the road to **Kallithea,** a village that extends to the right and to the left of the main road and is full of orchards and olive groves, or go on to **Skoulikado,** a Zakynthian village with a rich cultural heritage. The cultural society of the village organises events, talks and traditional Zakynthian theatrical plays throughout the year. You can visit the **Church of the Virgin Mary of Anafonitrias in Skoulikado**, built on a natural terrace overlooking the plain. The tower-like belfry rises to a height of 34 m, thus showing

Alikanas. The beach that is situated to the south of the Bay of Alykes

everyone where the village is. At the edge of the village stands the **Church of Ag. Nikolaos of Megalomati**. To go into the courtyard of the church you have to pass under the arch of the stone belfry. Entering the church our eyes are immediately drawn to the icon of Ag. Nikolaos impressed on the floor next to the iconostasis. Legend has it that it was discovered as we see it today;

The windless Bay of Alykes with its salt-pans and small anchorage where the green vegetation reaches the sea

the only thing that the human hand added was the silver border around the icon.

A small detour leads us to **Ag. Marina.** The old school of the village can be found in the courtyard of the church, and is a characteristic sample of Zakynthian architecture. A small square-like cell still stands on the other side, dated 1912, where insane persons from the island and other regions were incarcerated. Inside the cell we see the thick chain that was passed among the feet of the "prisoners". Before the cell was built, the chain –together with the slab of rock that it was attached to– was placed at the back of the church. It was here that the insane were tied because it was believed that Ag. Marina would heal them. The homonymous church and

its courtyard have been declared a preserved monument. The Church of Ag. Marina that we see today was built in 1855 on the site where the old church –built in 1643– used to stand. The wood-carved iconostasis inside the church belonged to the old church. The Virgin Mary on the iconostasis is an old icon by G. Vidali dating back to 1680. The interior of the church is adorned with four pairs of imposing one-piece stone columns with a height of about 6 meters and a circumference of 1.85 m.

These columns were all made from one piece of rock that had been found in the region of Koutoufasi in 1855. The belfry, which had been destroyed by the earthquake, was rebuilt by local craftsmen using original stones where possible and faithfully following the form and adornment of the old one. Climbing its spiral stairs, you have an amazing view from the top. The plain, the Bay of Alykes and the town are all spread out before you, as far as the eye can see.

The rood that passes right next to the foot of the hill –which is why the villages that we come across in the region are called foot villages– continues southwards towards the villages of **Ag. Pantes, Fiolitis, Langadakia** and terminates at Macherado. At this time we again turn

in the direction of the plain and reach Ag. Dimitrios after passing through the Settlement of **Drakas.** The next large village is **Ag. Kirykos,** where on our left is a small obelisk, a monument to those patriots who died in the battle to liberate Greece during

The historical Monastery of Anafonitrias; the defensive 15th C. tower stands at its entrance

the Second World War. On the main road above the small square is the Church of Ag. Kirykos, built just before the earthquake. On June 15th the village celebrates the Saint with a traditional festival and much revelry. Just before we reach the village, we meet **Sarakinado.** In the square of the village is the Church of Ag. Nikolaos, which hosts the iconostasis from the Church of Ag. Ioannis of Prodromos situated inside the Kastro. We pass through the villages of **Vanato** and **Gaitani** and soon reach our starting point, the town of Zakynthos.

Zakynthos – Orthonies
Askos – Volimes – Korithi
Ag. Nikolaos – Makrys Gialos

5th EXCURSION

The mountainous village of Volimes, known for its handmade textiles

With this 5th Excursion we complete our tour of Zakynthos. The north-eastern part of the island that we will now explore is enchanting and multifarious. The new road helps us to cover the distance more quickly, more enjoyably and more safely. We begin our tour from Alykes, which we had reached during our 4th Excursion. The first stop that we make is at the **Monastery of Ioannis of Prodromos** situated at the foot of the mountain. Built in the 16th C., the church of the monastery contains remarkable samples of ecclesiastical art, such as the iconostasis and the icon of Ag. Ioannis. The Zakynthian stone belfry raises its cross into the heavens. The view from here hugs the sea, reaches Cephalonia and the mountains of the Peoponnese. We return to the main road and head towards **Orthonies**, a small highlands village situated amphitheatrically on the slope of Vrachiona. In the square of the village we see the **Church of Archangelon Gavriil and Michail.** From Orthonies a road lead us to the **Monastery of the Virgin Mary of Spiliotissas**, founded in the middle of the 16th C. The monastery took its name from the icon of the

The Monastery of the Virgin Mary of Spiliotissa contains an impressive wood-carved iconostasis

Virgin Mary that was discovered inside a cave on the other side of the mountain.

The new road linking Alykes with Ag. Nikolaos tempts us to detour around **mountainous Volimes** and continue along the coast. However, if we have the time, it is worth visiting the villages in northern Zakynthos that, since they are quite far from the centre and have been relative untouched by tourism, they still preserve a sense of enchantment.

We therefore continue on towards Volimes and leave our visit to the shores in the region for another time. The road winds uphill until after a sharp bend we come across the stone houses of the village that are in harmony with the untamed landscape. **Volimes** is famous for its **well-made textiles** and lace that are made by the women of the Agricultural Cooperative. On the road the locals also sell –other than textiles- **oil-cheese, wine and honey**. Volimes is actually comprised of three smaller settlements: Ano, Kato and Meso Volimes. On entering the village, we take the left road leading to Meso and Kato Volimes. The **Church of Ag. Paraskevi**

Magical coloured palettes can be found throughout the trip

*The Church of Agia Paraskevi with its belfry that is similar
to that of Ag. Dionysios in the Chora*

stands out among the carefully built whitewashed houses with their yards shadowed by vine arbours. The church dates back to 1633, while its belfry is an exact copy of the belfry of Ag. Dionysios. A road from Meso Volimes leads to Cape Skinari and the Galazio Spileo (=Blue Cave).

Leaving Kato Volimes we carry on to the ruined **Monastery of Ag. Andreas,** built next to an abrupt cliff. The frescoes that adorned the church of the monastery have a place of honour among the exhibits at the Museum for Post-Byzantine Art in the town. The view from where the monastery is situated is phantasmagorical. On a small islet stands the Chapel of Ag. Andrea, from which the islet derived its name.

The steep rocky shores of Western Zakynthos begin from Cape Skinari

From Volimes we pass though the Settlement of **Korithi** and continue on our excursion towards the northern-most cape of Zakynthos, that of **Skinari** and Galazio Spileo. On reaching Skinari, we can tour the renowned **Galazio Spileo** with a caique, which was formed by continuous land erosions that created magnificent stone arches. The reflection of the light inside the cave paints everything an intense blue. The best time to visit the

The sky-blue caves form an enchanting picture. Daylight creates a fantastic blue-green coloured sea

Galazio Spileo is early in the morning when the light gives off its best possible hues.

The road to the right after Korithi leads us to the small port of Ag. Nikolaos. Guarding the entrance to the port is the **small Islet of Ag. Nikolaos**, where we can discern the ruins of the Monastery of Ag. Nikolaos. The beach, with its pebbles and small rocks, attracts quite a few people who want to swim in its clear waters and visit the caves. During the summer months ferry-boats depart from Ag. Nikolaos for Cephalonia and caiques for Navagio.

We can also combine our swimming with a visit to the **Petrino Parko of Askou.** A small detour will take us to the specially created Parko (Park) where many animals and birds live un-caged in their natural habitat. Other than the animals, there is also a remarkable variety of flora to see, with over 170,000 natural plants, bushes and trees of Zakynthos.

Returning to the main road, we can stop at the Beach of **Makry Gialou** to enjoy our swim in the cool and clean waters of the sea. Caves have formed in the rocks to the right of the beach which you can reach either by swimming or renting a paddle-boat or canoe.

The return trip back to the town is very short as we continue straight along the road to Alykes and from there via **Vanatou** we return back to our starting point.

You can admire all the flora and fauna of Zakynthos while visiting the Petrino Park of Askou

120-121: Makrys Gialos – Another wonderful sandy beach in mountainous Zakynthos

ΝΗΣΟΣ ΖΑΚΥΝΘΟΣ
ZAKYNTHOS ISLAND

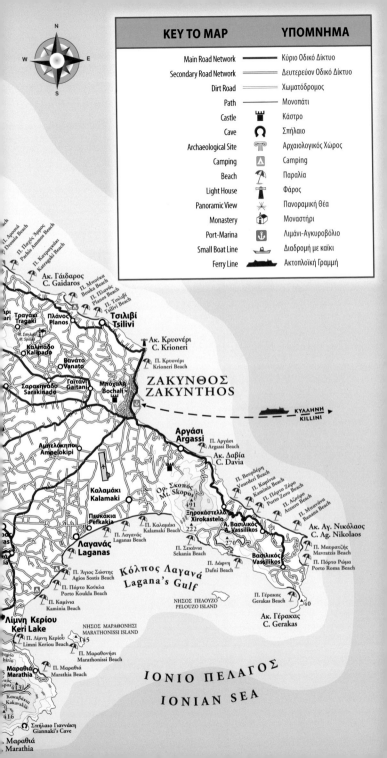

HOTELS

ZAKYNTHOS (TOWN)

ALBA	26950 26641
LINA	26950 28531
STRADA MARINA	26950 42761
ANDRIANA	26950 28149
AEGLI	26950 28317
APOLLON	26950 42838
BITZARO	26950 23644
DIANA	26950 28547
GARDELINO	26950 44333
KRYONERI	26950 23567
PALATINO	26950 27780
PHOENIX	26950 42419
PLAZA	26950 48909
REPARO	26950 23578
YRIA	26950 44682
ANTZELA	26950 51195
DIETHNES	26950 22286
IONION	26950 22511
OMONIA	26950 22113
DESSY	26950 28505
OLYMPIA	26950 28328

AGRILIA

AGRILIA	26950 51884

ARGASI

DIANA PALACE	26950 23070
KATERINA PALACE	26950 26998
PORTO YLIESSA	26950 27800
ZAKANTHA BEACH	26950 26441
CAPTAIN'S	26950 42779
CHRYSSI AKTI	26950 28679
CONTESA	26950 45152
ELEANA	26950 42895
MIMOSA BEACH	26950 42588
PALMYRA	26950 25707
PARADISE BEACH	26950 23620
YLIESSA	26950 45345
ADMIRAL	26950 42779
ANEMOMYLOS	26950 28230
ARGASSI BEACH	26950 48094
CASTELLO	26950 23520
COMMODORE	26950 26163
FAMILY INN	26950 45359
GAZEBO INN	26950 42300
IONION HILL	26950 26203
KRINAS	26950 41370
LEVANTE	26950 42833
LOKANDA	26950 45563
MIRABELLE	26950 45676
PIGHASSOS	26950 23070

BOCHALI

VARRES	26950 28352
ZANTE PALACE	26950 49090
AKROTIRI	26950 48000
LOFOS STRANI	–

GAITANI

PARK	26950 23790

KALAMAKI

MEANDROS	26950 49065
BITZARO PALACE	26950 45773
DENNY'S INN	26950 27785
EXOTICA	26950 27740
GOLDEN SUN	26950 49074
KALAMAKI BEACH	26950 42575
KLELIA	26950 27056
MARELEN	26950 26137
SIROKOS	26950 26083
VENUS	26950 27459
ANAGENESSIS VILLAGE	26950 45115
CAVO D'ORO	26950 22451
CRYSTAL BEACH	26950 42774
DANIEL	26950 26094
GARDEN VILLAGE APTS	26950 27139
GHIANNIS & ZOE	26950 27795
KALIDONIO	26950 44237
LOUROS BEACH	26950 23025
METAXA	26950 27441
RANIA	26950 27874
SOFIA	–
VANESSA	26950 26713

KATASTARI

ASTORIA	26950 83533
IONIAN STAR	26950 83416
MONTREAL	26950 83241
ASTERIA	26950 83203

TRAGAKI

PLAGOS BEACH	26950 62429
AMBOULA BEACH	26950 62387

LITHAKIA

PORTO KOUKLA BEACH	26950 52391
ZANTE SUN	26950 52320
BOZIKIS PALACE	26950 52260
GLORIA MARIS	26950 51546
DIVINA	26950 28587

MOUZAKI

OSKAR	26950 51990
PORTEGO	–
YAKINTHOS	26950 51211

LAGANAS

ASTIR PALACE	26950 53300
ZANTE PARK	26950 51948
ASTIR	26950 51730
CALIFORNIA BEACH	26950 51392
GALAXY	26950 51171
LAGANAS	26950 51793
MEGAS ALEXANDROS	26950 51580
PALACE	26950 51805
POSEIDON BEACH	26950 51189
ZANTE BEACH	26950 51130
ZANTE HOTEL	26950 51611
ALKYONIS	26950 51194
AUSTRALIA	26950 51071
BLUE COST	26950 22287
CACTUS	–
CASTELLI	26950 52367
ESPERIA	26950 51505
EUGENIA	26950 51149
GALAZIA KYMATA	26950 51791
GIANNOPOULOS BEACH	–
HELLINIS	26950 51164
I HARA TIS THALASSAS	26950 51992
IKAROS	26950 52290
ILIOS	26950 48911
IONIS	26950 51141
KANANDIA	–
MARGARITA	26950 51534
OLYMPIA	26950 51644
PANORAMA	26950 51144
PARASKEVI	26950 28361
PERKE	26950 51758
SELINI	26950 51154
SIRENE	26950 51188
SISSY	26950 52266
VESAL	26950 51155
VICTORIA	26950 51617
VYZANTION	26950 51136
ZANTE PARK II	26950 52310
GALAZIA THALASSA	26950 51123
NATALI	26950 52394
VIVIAN	26950 51705

ALYKANAS

VALAIS	26950 83223
DANNY'S HOTEL	–
KALI PIGHI	26950 83075

LETSOS	26950 83760
VILLA SANTA MONICA	26950 83550

PANTOKRATORAS

ARCHONTIKO GIANNAKOU	26950 51940

PLANOS (TSILIVI)

CARAVEL ZANTE	26950 45541
PHOENIX BEACH	26950 22483
ST. DENNIS	26950 45296
MAVRIKOS	26950 45907
MEDITERANNE	26950 26100
ALEXANDRA BE	26950 26190
ANETIS	26950 28899
CONTESSINA	26950 22508
COSMOPOLITE	26950 28752
DIAS	26950 48015
OREA HELENI	26950 28788
PARADISSOS	26950 45096
TEREZA	26950 24500
TSILIVI	26950 23110

ROGIA

TSAMIS ZANTE	26950 61659

VASILIKOS

GOLDEN BAY VILLAGE	26950 35435
PALAZZO DI ZANTE	26950 35121
ZANTE ROYAL PALACE I	26950 35492
ZANTE ROYAL PALACE II	26950 35492
ZANTE ROYAL PALACE III	26950 35492
AQUARIUS	26950 35300
MATILDA	26950 35376
STAMIRIS	–
VASSILIKON BEACH	26950 24114
PORTO ROMA	26950 22781

VOLIMES

BLUE BEACH	26950 27013
LA GROTTA	26950 31224

ALYKES

ALYKES PARK	26950 83592
CONSTANTINOS	26950 83060
GALINI	26950 83264

USEFUL INFORMATION

• How to reach the island

By Plane   Zakynthos has a regular air link with Athens, daily in summer and many times a week during the rest of the year. The trip lasts 50-55 minutes and Zakynthos Airport is situated in Laganas, 6 km from the town of Zakynthos. We can travel from the airport to the town by taxi or the Olympic Airways (O.A.) shuttle-bus.

Information:	O.A. Athens:	210-9666666
	O.A. Zakynthos:	26950-28611, 42617
	Zakynthos Airport:	26950-28322

By Bus and Ferry-Boat   There is a daily service by the KTEL Zakynthos Bus Service to the port in Kyllini in Ilia, a distance of 286 km from Athens. There are direct services to Zakynthos. The trip lasts a total of 6 hours (4.5 hours by bus and 1.5 hours by ferry-boat).

Information:	Athens KTEL Bus Station:	210-5129432
	Zakynthos KTEL Bus Station:	26950-42656, 22255
	Kyllini Port Authority:	26230-92211
	Zakynthos Port Authority:	26950-42417

By Train   There is also a daily train service from Athens to Kavasila in Ilia, and from there by ferry-boat.

Information:	Athens OSE Train Station:	210-5131601
	Pyrgos Ilias OSE Train Station:	26210-22576

Links between Zakynthos and other Places

Zakynthos is linked by ferry-boat with other places such as Mytika in Mainland Greece, Lefkada and Cephalonia.

• Useful Telephone Numbers (26950-):

Tourist Police:	24482, 24484
General Hospital:	42514-5
Zakynthos Hotel Association:	22779
Radio-taxi	48400
Police	42008